Edward Bayley

Remarks on certain dates occurring on the coins of the

Hindu kings of Kul

.

Edward Bayley

Remarks on certain dates occurring on the coins of the Hindu kings of Kul

ISBN/EAN: 9783337279769

Hergestellt in Europa, USA, Kanada, Australien, Japan

Cover: Foto ©Andreas Hilbeck / pixelio.de

Weitere Bücher finden Sie auf **www.hansebooks.com**

REMARKS ON CERTAIN

DATES OCCURRING ON THE COINS

OF THE

HINDU KINGS OF KABUL,

EXPRESSED IN THE GUPTA ERA AND IN ARABIC
(OR QUASI-ARABIC) NUMERALS.

BY

SIR E. CLIVE BAYLEY, K.C.S.I.

REPRINTED FROM THE NUMISMATIC CHRONICLE,
VOL. II., THIRD SERIES, PAGES 128—165.

LONDON:
1882.

REMARKS ON CERTAIN DATES OCCURRING ON THE COINS OF THE HINDU KINGS OF KÁBUL, EXPRESSED IN THE GUPTA ERA AND IN ARABIC (OR QUASI-ARABIC) NUMERALS.

By Sir E. Clive Bayley, K.C.S.I.

SHORTLY after the appearance of Mr. Edward Thomas's Paper on the "Coins of the Hindu Kings of Kabul," which was published in 1848, that gentleman communicated to me his belief that certain signs which occur before the head of the horseman, found on one type of these coins, represented dates. More recently he informed me that on some of the *later* coins, he believed that he could discover among these signs, a degraded and contracted form of the word "Gupta."

I have only recently been able to go through my own collection of this class of coins, and to compare it with the extensive series in the British Museum and in the India Office. I have also had the advantage of access to the collections of Mr. C. J. Rodgers and Mr. A. Grant; and it may be said at once, that the results obtained seem not only to confirm Mr. Thomas's conjectures, but to go considerably beyond them.

It is proposed, therefore, in the following pages to deal with these results; and, in order to place the matter clearly before the reader, it is intended to adopt the following method :—First, to relate concisely the facts themselves—

a

both those now discovered, and those already known—
which bear upon the subject discussed. Secondly, to state
simply the conclusions drawn ; and, in the third place, to
set out the evidence on which the new facts rest; and,
finally, to give the reasoning by which the conclusions
drawn are supported.

The facts then are briefly these :—

I. There exist (as read by me) dates on certain silver
coins of the bull-and-horseman type, and the coins on
which these dates occur all bear the name of "Syalapati,"
whom Mr. Thomas has shown to have been the earliest
king of the *Brahminical* line of Kábul kings. In some
cases these dates are followed by the word "Gupta"
(possibly the full legend is "Guptasya (kál)," for another
letter appears on some coins after "Gupta ").   All these
coins which bear either dates with the full word "Gupta,"
or nearly contemporary dates, are assumed to have been,
both from their dates and their execution, struck by Syalapati *himself*.

II. On certain other coins of the same general type,
but of distinctly conventional execution, and which bear
the names of Syalapati and Samanta (in rare cases the
names of Bhíma Deva and Khvadavayaka) indiscrimi-
nately *other* dates occur, which if I read them correctly,
belong to a period about a century later than the dates on
the earlier coins.   This class of coins it is proposed to
consider posthumous, and as belonging to the latest and
subordinate kings of the dynasty, to whom the privilege
of coining in their own names had been forbidden (as
would usually be the case) by their Mahomedan con-
querors and superior rulers.

III. In the British Museum is a coin which bears on
one side the conventional lion or leopard of the early or

" Túrk " type,[1] that found on " Varka Deva's " coins,
but on the other is a peacock of the form found on the
small silver coins of the Gupta dynasty. Above the lion
is a Hindi legend, which is either " Sri Kamara " or
" Kamra " (Deva?), possibly it may stand for "Kúmára ; "
but in any case the name seems easily identifiable, as the
original of " Kamlua," the name given in the " Jami-
ul-Hikayát" to the "King of India," there described as
the opponent of Amrú Lais, who flourished between 878
and 900 A.D.[2]

IV. In my own collection is found the name of another
king, " Padama " or " Padma," [3] and since the type of his
(copper) coin is precisely similar to that of Varka Deva,
the last king of the Túrk dynasty, there need be little
hesitation in assigning to this king a place before "Varka"
and after " Kamara."

V. There is further still in my collection, by the gene-
rosity of Mr. C. J. Rodgers, a copper coin of Samanta
Déva—imitated from those of " Varka," as certain of his
coins are already known to be, and which bears above
the lion an Arabic legend, which it is proposed to read
as " Al Mutaki " (or Al Muttaki) B'illah, being the name
of the Khalif who reigned from 940 to 944 A.D. On the
other side is the name of Samanta himself. I may add
that I possess another coin of Samanta of this type which
bears another and totally different Arabic legend, unfor-

---

[1] The reading of " Varka Deva" is adopted, in conformity
with Mr. Thomas's reading, but I believe that gentleman, and
General Cunningham also, now prefer to read " Vakka."
" Vanka " is closer the rendering of Mahomedan writers, and
each reading may be supported by the coins.
[2] Elliot, " Mahomedan Historians of India," vol. ii. p. 423.
[3] The second letter of the name is badly formed, and might
be possibly a " k," but I think it should be " d."

tunately the coin is in poor preservation, and the legend cannot be fully deciphered. It does not, however, seem to contain a name, and so does not bear directly on the present inquiry.

These are the chief new facts, on which, in addition to those already made known by Mr. Thomas [especially the existence of the Khalif Al-Muktadir's name on a coin of the bull-and-horseman type, and Albirúni's account of the fall of the "Túrk," and rise of the Brahminical dynasty] the conclusions about to be stated, mainly rest.

These conclusions are as follows :—

1. It is proposed to read the dates as being written in numerals of a form intermediate between those of the mediæval Indian mints and the modern Arabic forms, and as graduating into the latter.

2. On this hypothesis the dates on the earlier coins — viz., those attributed to Syalapati himself—would read as,[4] '98, and perhaps '99, Gupta (Sya?) ; and as 707 and 727 (Gupta). Of course, if correct, these readings would give Syalapati a reign of at least twenty-nine years, which is not à priori very improbable.

3. On the same hypothesis, the dates on the later series of coins are read as 802 "Gu," 812 "Gu," 813, 814, 815, and 817, respectively. A still later date of 886 occurs also on a single (copper) coin of a degraded type.

4. The identification of "Kamara" with Kamlua makes it necessary to place part at least of the reign of that king, and the whole of the reign of "Padma," and the whole of the first reign of Varka Deva between 878 A.D., the earliest year of Amrú Lais, and the date

---

[1] Such a reading is justified by the Hindi dates for (6)97, (6)98, (6)99, which occur on coins of a Ala-ud-din Khilji of Dehli.

of Syalapati's accession to the throne. The first reign of " Varka " must have been one of some duration, for the accounts given by Mahomedan writers describe him as going through varied phases of behaviour before he was finally dethroned.

5. The reading of the name of " Al Mutaki b'illah " on one coin of Samanta makes it clear that Samanta was ruling at least as early as 944 A.D., the latest year of that Khalif; and this makes it certain also that Syalapati's reign must have terminated at a distinctly earlier date, for Varka's second reign interposed between those of Syalapati and Samanta. Now though Varka's second reign can hardly have been a *very* long one—for if Syalapati ruled for some thirty years or more, Varka must have been at a fairly advanced age when he regained his throne on Syalapati's death; still it must have been of some sensible duration, inasmuch as the type of Varka's coinage, which had pretty certainly been entirely disused during the time Syalapati was on the throne, had regained sufficient acceptance among the people to induce Samanta to imitate it in his copper currency, while taking Syalapati's type for his silver coinage.

6. From the above considerations it is clear that Syalapati was contemporary at least for some time with the Khalif, " Al Muktadir b'illah," and that he was probably the king who struck the medal (published by Mr. Thomas) in his honour, of the bull-and-horseman type. Al Muktadir reigned from 907-8 to 932 A.D.

7. Dr. Bühler[5] has pointed out that at Vallabhi, when visited by the Chinese traveller, Hwen Thsang, in 641 A.D., a king was then reigning, whose appellation has

[5] " Indian Antiquary," vol. vii. p. 80.

been already rendered by earlier modern interpreters into
a name closely resembling Dhruvabháta, as its Sanskrit
equivalent ; and a recently discovered inscription of
Siladitya VI., of Gújerat, dated in 447, gives to that king
the title of "Dhruvabháta." No other king of Valabhi,
so far as their known inscriptions show (and many grants
of nearly all his predecessors are now known), adopted
any similar title. His immediate predecessor, Siladity V.,
was reigning in 441. For reasons to be explained presently the era of these dates is taken as the Gupta era :
if so, this would limit the latest possible date of the commencement of the Gupta era to 200 A.D.

8. Dr. Beal in "J. R. A. S.," vol. xiii. N.S. p. 571,
gives a quotation from a Chinese author, who, writing
slightly later than 692 A.D., speaks of a king of India
called "Sri Gupta," who reigned "about five hundred
years ago." The earliest king of the Gupta dynasty was
"Sri Gupta."

9. For these reasons it is proposed to place the extreme latest limit of the commencement of the Gupta era
in 200 A.D.

10. On the other hand, taking 698 Gupta as the earliest
date of Syalapati known, this must, as has been shown,
fall much later than 878 A.D. ; and therefore 180 A.D. would
be certainly too early a date for the commencement of the
Gupta era.

11. Samanta Deva reigned probably for a long period.
His name occurs perhaps more frequently than Syalapati's
on the Kábul coins of later date ; and it is the only one
associated with the bull-and-horseman type, by the kings
of later Hindu dynasties, and by the Mahomedans who
imitated *their* coinage.

12. The long duration of the reigns of Syalapati and of

Samanta and the uncertain length of Varka Deva's second and intervening reign, make it difficult to fix their period more exactly from the above data, and from it to settle positively the initial date of the Gupta era. If, however, a date about half-way between the extreme limits be taken—viz. 189—which, as will be seen presently, suits fairly well with other known facts, then it would give the following results, which are not improbably correct, at least approximately.

A.D.

I. Kamara or Kamlua, contemporary with Amru Lais . . . . ⎫
II. Padama or Pakma . . . . ⎬ 878 to 887
III. Varka Deva's first reign . . . ⎭
IV. Syalapati . . . . . . 887 to 916
V. Varka Deva, second reign, say ten years 916 to 926
VI. Samanta Deva . . . . circa 926
and at least until . . . 940

13. The peculiar character of the numerals used on the coins shows, it will be affirmed, that the Arabic numerals were not only derived from India (as is already known), but also *through the medium of Hindus of the Kábul.*

The above conclusions have in some cases been put in an argumentative form, but this has been done in order to make their connection clear. It will now be necessary to go back to the evidence of the facts alleged, and to explain more fully the arguments by which the conclusions stated have been derived from these facts, and, finally, to consider the objections to which these conclusions may seem open, and which arise from other data or presumed data.

In the first place, then, reference must be made to the accompanying plates of coins, and it will be convenient to deal first with the group which bear Arabic inscriptions.

The coin bearing the name of Al Muktadir-billah needs no
further notice here, as it has been already dwelt upon by
Mr. Thomas in his original paper.   The coin on which
the name of Al Mutáki is read is shown in Pl. I., as
figured 15.   For the reading of the first three letters as
"alif," "lám," and "mím," respectively, there is ample
authority; and indeed the same may be said of the final
"yé;" the penultimate letter may well be "Káf" ﮐ
though it might also stand for either "mím," or "fé."
The real difficulty of the reading lies in the "t," which is
only represented by a straight line between the "m," and
the antepenultimate letter, instead of by a line with a slight
upward projection; but the letters, which are evidently
Arabic, can hardly form any other probable word, and
the error may be that of a foreign die-cutter, unaccus-
tomed to Arabic writing.   There is a group of four dots
arranged in a lozenge over the latter part of the legend,
which may be intended as a fanciful arrangement of diacritical points, though the omission of these was certainly
not unusual at the period when the coin must have been
struck; or it may be a mere ornament, for such groups of
dots occur on other coins of the same type.   If, however,
they are taken as diacritical marks, these dots çan only be
divided, so as to make sense, by taking them in groups of
two dots each, which would give the reading "Al Mutaki."

  [6] The other coins of Syalapati with Arabic inscriptions,
though some are well preserved—and they are fairly
numerous—have not been fully deciphered: the only word
clearly legible is the name of "Mahomed."   In all pro-

---

  [6] There are four specimens in the B.M. Collection, two in my
own, and one in that of Mr. Rodgers; two also in the E.I. Office
Collection.   Two of the former and that of Mr. Rodgers are
engraved as figures 11, 12, and 13.

bability the legend will be found merely to contain some pious Mahomedan formula, and the numismatic value of these coins, as well as of all of those with other unread Arabic inscriptions, consists mainly in the evidence which they afford of the strength of Mahomedan domination in Kábul during the reign of Syalapati, and of his immediate successors; evidence which is wholly in accord with the facts, stated at more or less length, by the whole series of Mahomedan writers, who deal with the period under review.[7]

---

[7] These facts will be found detailed at length in the note by Sir Henry Elliot, in vol. ii. pp. 403 to 437 of the " Mahomedan Historians of India," and by Mr. Edward Thomas in his papers on the Hindu kings of Kábul, already quoted, and on the coins of the kings of Ghazni, J.R.A.S., vol. ix. O.S.   Briefly to summarize the leading facts, so far as they affect the present question, it may be said that attacks by the Mahomedans upon the Hindus of Kábul are recorded as early as the year 33 A.H., and they were repeated with varying success till 107 A.H.; after which the country of Kábul is described as being a permanent dependency of the Mahomedans. In the middle of the third century A.H. Yakúb-bin-Lais took the city of Kábul, and about a quarter of a century later Amrú Lais, his son, was, as has been seen, again in hostile contact with the Kábul king; and just about the time when it is proposed to place Syalapati's rule, the fortress of the city of Kábul (possibly the Bala Hissár of to-day) was, according to Istakhri, held by a Moslem garrison. A little later Ibn Haukal gives a similar account, and adds that it was the Moslem outpost on the frontier of India, and that nevertheless the Hindu sovereigns of Kábul were not considered as lawfully instituted, unless instituted in Kábul itself, a fact which implies at any rate some kind of subjection to the Mahomedan power. In short, between the beginning and the middle of the tenth century A.D.,—just the period assigned to Syalapati and his immediate successors—the country was in the military possession and under the supremacy of the Mahomedans. Twenty-five years later this modified tenure of the country was apparently converted into entire administrative possession, for the kingdom of Jaipál, who was reigning at least as early as 975 A.D., is described as extending no further to the westward than Lamghan, and he was, doubtless, soon pushed further still to the south-east.

As regards the coins of Kamara and Padama, Figs. 1 and 2, Pl. I., no more need be said. The Hinduized form of these names, if correctly read, need not excite astonishment, though borne by the so-called "Túrk" race (if indeed the Katórs, or Katormáns, were Túrks), for the third king of the Kanishka Indo-Scythian dynasty was "Vúsu Déva."

It is now necessary to explain the readings of the dated coins, and the word "Gupta" first claims attention. The most perfect example will be found on the coin, Fig. 3, Pl. I.; but even on this coin the syllable which I read as "Gu" is partially effaced, as are all the numerals preceding it. The full reading given as Fig. 6, Pl. I., is compiled from the three coins, Figs. 3, 4, and 5, Pl. I., and it will be perhaps accepted as a fair rendering of the usual form of the word; and though the letters are slightly more archaic than those of the rest of the legend on some of Syalapati's coins, still a few of these legends retain an early form of "y," and are otherwise pretty closely in accord with the form in which "Gupta" is given, and which was perhaps to some extent stereotyped.[8]

The general type of these coins likewise demands attention. If the figure of the horse on these coins be compared with that on the coins which have been described as "posthumous," as, for example, the figures 25 to 33, Pl. II., it will probably be admitted that while the more or less rude outlines on the latter give only a general conception of a horse, the figure on the early dated coin gives a fairly faithful representation of the short thick "punchy"

---

[8] Since this was written Mr. Thomas has kindly permitted me to see his notes and facsimiles. The last letter seems from these to be probably "sa" or "sya," which would make the whole word "Guptasya" (kid).

horse, to this day indigenous in Kábul, and bears every mark of having been taken from a living original. The same is, in a less degree, true of the figure of the bull, for although as it was doubtless a representation of the sacred bull Nandi, and was therefore from the first more or less formalized, still on a few of the early coins of Syalapati it retains some approach to nature, and, in one or two instances, the coins even show the bull as in the act of rising.

As regards the numerals, the readings proposed will be seen at a glance on reference to the table at the end of Plate II. Those of Syalapati's earlier coins will be found in columns 6, 7, and 8, which give the variants found on that series of coins ; while columns 9, 10, and 11 give most of those found on the later coins, but do not show all the more corrupted forms of the Figure 4, which are numerous. In the earlier columns of the table will be found a series of ancient Indian numerals, viz., the earliest, the Gupta, and the later Valabhi forms, together with some of those on the bilingual coins (Sanskrit and Arabic) of Mahmúd of Ghazni, and the modern Hindi ; the concluding columns give the modern Arabic and Persian forms ; while, outside the table, will be found examples of the modes of writing 100, 200, 300, 400, according to the Valabhi system, which does not, however, essentially differ from the earlier modes of expressing the same numbers.

To this table it will only be necessary to add a few words of explanation. It has been conclusively shown by M. de Woepcke, in the "Journal Asiatique," vol. i., Series 6, for 1863, that the Arabs received their numerals from India, and the early writers indeed (Albirúni, for example) always designate what we now call the "Arabic" as "Indian" numerals. The object of the remarks it is

now proposed to offer is to indicate the gradations by
which the ancient Indian numerals passed into the modern
Arabic forms, as will be shown by the table given, and to
attempt an explanation of the more important changes
made in these forms which it is believed can be traced to
the action of the Hindus of Kábul; through whom, therefore, it may without danger be assumed that the knowledge of these ciphers was first brought from India to the
Arabs, and this from the geographical position and political
relations of the two nations is à priori probable.[9]

Passing over the earlier units for the present, which
will be more conveniently dealt with in connection with
the later coins, it may be observed that no early example
of the cipher for " 6," can be positively adduced from the

---

[9] M. de Woepcke shows that up to 705 A.D., and possibly for
some seventy years later, the Arabs certainly possessed no numerals of their own, and he quotes two passages from Arabic writers
which record explicitly the reception of a system of numeration
from India, through the medium of a book or books presented
to the reigning Khalifs, 773 A.D., by envoys from India. From
the stress laid on the beautiful simplicity of this system, it may
perhaps be not unfairly inferred that the system recorded was
the modern system, for the system of notation by the Greek
letters is not very greatly inferior to the earlier Indian method.
The new system was certainly known and employed in India
by that time, though the older one remained in use for a much
later period in Nipál and other remote places. It is not
necessary in this place to deal with M. de Woepcke's arguments
tending to assign a much earlier date to the simplification of the
system of notation. These are mainly derived from the use of
the value of position; but this was only one element of the new
discovery, and probably the earliest part in point of time. See
the observations of M. Leon Rodet at the close of the "avant-
propos " to his paper on the notation of Aryabhata, p. 443, vol.
xvi. Series 7, "Journal Asiatique " for 1880. I hope, in another
place, shortly to show that the final simplification was hardly
effected much before the close of the seventh century A.D., and
to indicate at least with some probability the method in which
it was brought about.

Kábul series itself. It first occurred to me to read the sign just above the horse's head on coins, Figs. 4 and 5, Pl. I., as "6," and it may possibly be intended to fulfil that function ; still it so closely resembles the left arm of the horseman, as shown on other coins of this series, that it would not be safe to take it as a numeral. As will be seen, however, the figure for "6" is found on a coin of not greatly later date, in its ultimate Arabic form, and that form was clearly derivable from the oldest Indian type of the numeral, by simply writing it cursively so as to obliterate the central loop ;[10] just as the European "6" is derived from the same original, and is obtained merely by the omission of the final down stroke.

The early figures for "7," indeed all the forms of "7" on the Kábul coins, are plainly also cursive forms of the ancient Indian equivalent : and indeed not unlike its shape in modern Hindi, while one form is very closely allied to the European shape.

The "8" of the earliest series of the Kábul coins is hardly a variation from the form used in the ancient Gupta inscriptions, and differs almost in a less degree from that employed in modern Hindi ; the mode in which these two ciphers for 7 and 8 respectively passed into their modern Arabic shapes will be discussed presently.

The figure for "9," as it occurs on the earlier Kábul coins, is closely allied to the form used in modern Hindi and to that in use on the coins of Mahmúd of Ghazni, and is altogether different from that used in modern Arabic. The latter is in close accordance with the European form, and clearly also borrowed from an Indian original, and in

[10] It occurs nearly in this form in the inscription from Samaugarh, in West India, dated in 755 A.D. Cf. *Indian Antiquary* for 1882, pp. 110-11.

particular follows very closely the model of that numeral used in the later Valabhi inscriptions.

The precise genealogy of the modern *Hindi* form of "9" is not very certain. Mr. Thomas believes it to be a differentiation of the cipher for "8," by an addition at the top, but the point may be left open for the present.

Then remains the all-important cipher for "0," which is simply a small circle, and is only a slight modification of the most ancient form of the oldest Indian "ten." It will be attempted to show (in a separate paper) in the Journal of the R. Asiatic Society that the invention of the "zero" originally grew out of the use of the Indian sign for "ten" to fill up the "place vide" on the "Arcus Pythagoreus," but it may have taken its ultimate shape from that of the sexagesimal zero of Ptolemy.

If this interpretation be accepted, then the readings on the early coins (of Syalapati) will be as follows :—Fig. 4, Pl. I. will read, 98 Gupta (or Gupta Kál); Fig. 5, Pl. I. will read, 99 "Gupta," while on the coins figured as Nos. 7 and 8, Pl. I., the figures, *read the reverse way*, will make 707 and 727. I do not propose here to examine the question as to the reversed position of these figures, which will be dealt with in connection with the dates on the later series of coins ; but it may be now said in conclusion, that on the data given above rests the main part of the case which it is the purpose of this paper to put forward. If the reading of the word "Gupta" on these coins, and the interpretation of the dates on them (for if the signs are accepted as numerals, they can, taken with the word "Gupta," be nothing but dates), and if the assignment of the coin of "Kamara," and the reading of the name of Al Mutaki b'illah, be all accepted, the initial date of the Gupta era can hardly be earlier than 188, or later than

214 A.D., and the additional deductions from the inscriptions of the two last Siladityas of Gújerat would further
limit the latest date to 200 A.D.

The figures on the more recent coins must be now considered; and taking Pl. II., Figures 24, 25, 26, 27,
28, 29, 30, 31, 32, 33, in connection with the table
given on Pl. II., columns 9, 10, 11, it will be seen that I
read them respectively as 8 0 2 "Gu," 8 1 2 "Gu," 8 1 3
(Gu?). 8 1 4, 8 1 5, and 8 1 7 respectively.

The reading of the earlier numerals, 1, 2, 3, 4, requires,
in the first place, to be explained. It will be seen that
the first is represented, as in the modern Arabic, by a
simple upright stroke; "2" is the same upright stroke
differentiated by a single side stroke to the right; "3,"
the same, differentiated by two side strokes, the second
being *superimposed* on the first side stroke. It will be
seen that these two last are almost identical with the
Arabic ٢ and ٣, which are indeed but the same ciphers
written more cursively. On the other hand, they differ
entirely from the modern Hindi, and from the European
forms, and do not in any way resemble the ancient
Indian forms for 2 and 3, from which the last named
were evidently derived, by simply writing without raising
the pen from the paper, and joining all the strokes.

The following explanation of the process by which the
Kábul and Arabic forms were derived may[11] be offered as,

---

[11] Perhaps, in order to match the stiffer and more upright forms
of the Indian alphabet as eventually introduced into Kábul. It
seems more probable, however, that the fundamental idea of
this system was derived from the upright stroke which stood
for "one" in the Bactrian system of numeration which certainly prevailed in Kábul before the introduction of Indian
notation. The period of the new invention is more doubtful.
The Bactrian alphabet and notation appear to have survived

at least, not improbable:—It seems to have been decided
to obtain a set of distinct signs to supersede the groups of
simple strokes before in use ; and, to this end, the mode of
differentiation which had formerly been used with the now
discarded symbols for 100 and 1,000, was applied to the
simple upright stroke used for " 1 "; with this difference
only, that for convenience of cursive writing the additional stroke in the case of the " 3 " was superimposed *on*
the first, instead of being separately placed below it, as
in the model from which it was derived.

That this was really the origin of these forms will
become almost certain if Fig. 29, Pl. II., and the " 4 "
in column 9 of the table of Pl. II. be examined. It will be
seen from these that the figure for " 4 " was clearly
obtained by superadding to the figure for 3 the old
Indian cipher for 4, just as that cipher was tied to the
cipher for 100 to make 400. As has been said above,
the Valabhi modes of writing 100, 200, 300, and 400
are shown to the right, outside the table on Pl. II.

The cipher given for five, " 5," is, it must be said,
derived only from a single coin, but it is very clear on
that example, and can hardly stand for anything else.
Moreover, it is easily convertible, by joining the two ends
with a back stroke, into the modern Arabic form shown
in col. 14 of the table in Pl. II. It seems to be a cursive
mode of writing the Valabhi cipher for five. The upper

during the Indo-Scythian rule—say, till nearly 200 A.D.   On
the other hand, Sassanian coins of the sixth century exhibit
Sanskrit letters which must have been brought *through* Kábul
from India.   Anyway this very artificial contrivance must have
preceded the simplification of the Indian system, for it would
hardly have been adopted when the convenient forms of the
later Indian symbols had become known, and these were certainly used at a very early date.

part (as sometimes the case in Valabhi inscriptions) being exaggerated and the lower part slightly contracted.

The figure for " 6 " is shown in its modern Arabic shape, in which it will be found on Fig. 35, Pl. II. This coin bears unmistakeably the date ΛΛ५, and is, it will be seen, a rude corruption of the bull-and-horseman type. It has on one side a scarcely recognizable figure of the bull ; while the hind quarters of the horse, in their most conventional shape, are even less easily perceived on the other.

This last coin is of far too late a type to fit the date 886, either in the Sáka or Vikramáditya era, while it is of too early a type to fit 886 A.H., by which date the bull-and-horseman type had been practically abandoned even in the Kángra Valley, where it lingered longest. It seems, therefore, only to suit the Gupta date, which if taken hypothetically as beginning in 189 A.D. would bring the coin to 1075 A.D., and this would be in the time of Ibrahím of Ghazni ; in that case the coin may be taken to be probably the production of a petty Hindu rebel, claiming, perhaps, descent from the ancient dynasty, in some remote part of the country.

It will be seen that it is proposed to read as the equivalent of " 8 " on these later coins a very different figure from that similarly read as 8 on the earlier coins, and whereas that resembled closely the old Hindi form of 8, this is the exact Arabic form of the same numeral.

To explain this it will be necessary to refer to the figure for 7 in column 8 of the table, which, it will be seen, is the same as one of those which occurs in the earlier coins, and it is found (in one coin only, however, Fig. 33, Pl. II.) in the later series of coins. It will be obvious that this figure closely assimilates to that of the earlier 8, *turned the opposite way ;* and both these forms easily lent them-

c

selves to a cursive mode of writing them by two straight
lines converging at an angle (as will indeed be seen from
the plates,[12] the "7" is sometimes actually so written[12]
on the earlier coins). The distinction between them
would then be maintained only by writing the 8 in
opposite direction to the 7, viz., with the angle turned
upwards; but at the period when even the latest of these
coins were struck the older form of 7 still apparently
survived; perhaps, in this instance, by accident.

Of the other coins figured on Pl. II., Fig. 34 is the coin
of a Kangra prince, probably of the beginning of the eighth
or end of the seventh century A H.;[13] certainly not later—
possibly earlier. This coin with those of Khvadavayaka,
Pl. I., Figs. 17 and 18; Bhíma Deva, Figs. 19 and 20; and
Mahomed, Masaud, and Modúd of Ghazni, Pl. II. Figs. 21,
22, and 23, are given for a reason which I now proceed to
state.

To Mr. Thomas I am indebted for the hints which first
suggested the present inquiry; and as the result at which
I have arrived differs from that which he has obtained from
the same data, it is right that I should state as clearly as
I can his objections to the explanation proposed by me,
and the grounds on which I venture to differ from him.

As to the bare fact that the syllable "Ga" for "Gupta"
is found on the later coins, I understand Mr. Thomas to
concur with me; though he would take the sign, which at
best is a gross corruption, as reading the opposite way to

---

[12] See Fig. 9, Plate I.

[13] This coin is anonymous. The coins of "Rúp Chand,"
which are the earliest yet found with a name, are of a somewhat later character, and all the still later coins bear some name.
Rúp Chand was contemporary with Firóz Toghlak of Delhi.
A coin in Mr. Rodgers's collection, very closely resembling the
coin figured, *seems* to bear the name of Altumsh.

that suggested by me, and I understand him to read all
the figures in the same direction—at any rate, all those
on the later groups of coins—*i.e.*, as running from the
horse's head towards its feet, with the heads of the figures
towards the margin of the coin, and as representing in
shapes more or less corrupt one uniform date, viz., 617,
which he considers to be the initial date, according to
the Gupta era, of Samanta's dynasty; and accepting
319 A.D., according to Albiruni's statement, as the actual
date of the Gupta era, would thus place Samanta's accession in 936 A.D. One main objection to my reading held
by Mr. Thomas, besides the weight of Albiruni's testimony, consists in the fact that the numerals, read as I
propose to do, would run in a direction different from the
legend on the other side of the coins, and from the
monograms on the same side; while by his reading a
uniform direction is maintained for all.[14]

Before proceeding to discuss these arguments I must
make one important admission, which may at first sight
seem to support Mr. Thomas's position; and in order
to illustrate which I have introduced certain of the coins
figured above, viz., those of Khvadavayaka, Figs. 17, 18,
Pl. I.; Bhíma Deva, Figs. 19 and 20, Pl. I.; the Kángra
coin, Fig. 34, Pl. II.; and also the coins of Mahomed,
Masaud, and Modúd.

---

[14] Mr. Thomas stated that he scarcely expected to find these
dates expressed entirely in Arabic characters, and attributes
the employment of these to the dominance of Mahomedan
power; but this fact is otherwise explained, if, as I have endea-
voured to prove above, the Arabs *received* their numerals from
India, directly *through* Kábul; and if the peculiarities of the
Arabic numerals have their origin in the indigenous peculiarities
which distinguished the Kábul system of numerals, with the
exception of some slight later modifications adopted principally
to facilitate rapid writing. (See pp. 514, 515, vol. xiii. J.R.A.S.,
N.S.

This admission is that one date at least, viz., 814, has been undoubtedly copied mechanically on later coins, just as the early English mints of Furrakhábád and Murshidábád reproduced for many successive years mechanical imitations of the rupee of Sháh Alam's nineteenth year. I do not pretend to give any explanation of the selection of this particular date, which on the hypothesis of 189 A.D., as the initial date of the Gupta era, would be equivalent to 1003 A.D. There may, of course, have been some special reason for its adoption, or it may have been a type accidentally taken as a model by Mahomedan or other mintmasters, and reproduced unintelligently as it became a standard form. Mr. Rodgers has pointed out to me that the successors of Zain-ul-Abidín, in Kashmír, copied for many years, mechanically, the reverse type of his silver coin, which contains, in words, the date of 842, though giving correctly their own names, and sometimes their own correct dates in numerals also, on the obverse of these coins.

Having, however, made this admission, it is necessary to explain why I have ventured to dissent from the skilled judgment of Mr. Thomas. In the first place, appeal may be made to the coins themselves on which Mr. Thomas accepts the numerals as representing a date. If it were possible to read the figures which it is proposed read 812 Gu, 813, and 814, as all varying forms of one same group, this can at least hardly be said of those read as 802 Gu, 815, and 817 ; while 886 is entirely and unmistakeably different, and it seems scarcely likely if such violent changes took place in the last number (or first, according to Mr. Thomas) of the group, that they should rarely extend to the second, and not at all to the third number. So far, therefore, as even the evidence of the later class of coins themselves is concerned, the evidence that the

groups of numerals on them represent *consecutive* groups
seems little capable of resistance ; and if so, then as the
change is almost wholly confined to one extreme of the
group, the other extremity must perforce represent the
number of the century.

But to this must be added the evidence of the earlier
series of coins, which, however, I do not understand Mr.
Thomas to accept. If the groups of numerals on those
without the word " Gupta " be accepted as numerals,
it is pretty certain that those on the coins with it must
also be so taken, and the dates of '98 and '99 Gupta, to
say nothing of those of 707 and 727, are entirely opposed
to the initial date of 319, which Mr. Thomas supports.

It is, however, to be remarked that this class of coins
would present on my supposition examples of dates written
in *both* directions.[15] But this in itself is no anomaly on
Indian, and specially on Hindu coins. For example, on
the gold coins of the Guptas themselves, the legends read
sometimes round the edge with the heads pointing out-
wards ; and, again, on the same coin, upright in the centre
of the coin—one letter piled perpendicularly over another.
On the Hindu coins of Kashmír the same thing occurs.
On the coins of Toramáua, for instance, the name of the
king on the obverse is written round the margin with the
heads of the letters pointing to the centre of the coin, and
on the reverse the legend reads across the diameter of the
coin. On an unpublished coin in my own cabinet of
Pravaraséna the name is written as Toramána's, while the
name of the mint " Gandara " (for " Gandhara " probably)
is written on the reverse, one letter over the other perpen-

---

[15] By my reading, however, the word " Gupta " or " Gu "
would in every case and on both classes of coins *follow* the
date. On Mr. Thomas's theory it would on the earlier coins
follow, on the later precede, the date.

dicularly; and on a coin of " Hirnya " (Hiranya?) in the possession of Mr. A. Grant, also unpublished, the name is written exactly in the reverse way to that on the coins of Toramána and Pravaraséna.

It has been necessary to defend the reading of the later coins suggested, rather in order to answer Mr. Thomas's arguments than to maintain the main argument of this paper; for, as has been before pointed out, the conclusions at which I have arrived rest wholly on the evidence of the earlier coins, and if that evidence is correctly rendered, it is conclusive against Albirúni's date of 319, as also against the readings of the later coins adopted by Mr. Thomas in accordance therewith.

I am not able apart from the dates to suggest an assignment to any particular king for these later coins or to interpret them, as seemed possible, by the monograms occurring on them, one of which at least appeared at first sight to favour a connection with the name of " Bhíma; " but the monograms are too numerous for the few names of the later kings, and indeed fit no other name but that of Bhíma (pàl). I may observe, however, that the date of 189 A.D., if accepted as the commencement of the Gupta era, would bring down the years 812, 814 of that era, to a date immediately succeeding the battle near Peshàwur in 1001 A.D., 392 A.H., in which Mahmúd defeated and captured Júipál. 815 Gupta would be equivalent on the same hypothesis to 1004 A.D. = 395 A.H., the date of the capture of Bhéra or Bhíra), which was one of his capital cities. 817 would be 1006 A.D. = 973 A.H., about which year the Hindu convert, whom Mahomed had left as Governor in the Indian possessions, must have apostatised and revolted; for he was overthrown by Mahomed in the following year. If this were so the later

series of co'ns would probably all be referable to the Bhéra
Mint, of which ꣿ or ꣿ "Bhí," may be the mint-mark.
This last coin being struck by a usurper, a rebel, and an
apostate, would naturally form no model for the use of the
Mahomedan mint masters; and as the coins of 815 are
very rare, the capture of Bhéra would probably have taken
place early in that year, and when the coin of 814 would
be the latest type freely current. (See Elliot, vol. ii.
pp. 438—441.)

As regards Albirúni and his authority, it is very certain
that his statement at any rate cannot apply to the era
used by the Guptas themselves on their coins, for they can
hardly have *used* an era dating from their own extinction.
If not, then what era could they have used? If they used
the Sáka era, and if the Kshatrapahs used the Vikramáditya
era (and[16] they pretty certainly used either that, or some

---

[16] Although the date of the Kshatrapah era is not exactly
within the province of the present paper, it is so important a
factor in all the calculations as to the chronology of this period,
that some of the reasons which appear to warrant the assertion
that it must have been, if not identical with, very nearly
approaching the Vikramáditya era are given here by way of a
note. (1.) Asóka Maurya certainly reigned over the territory
which the Kshatrapahs subsequently possessed till *about* 225 B.C.
He was certainly followed by a crowd of Græco-Bactrian and
Parthian, if not also Indo-Scythian kings, to whom it is not too
much to assign a period of a century and three quarters, or even
two centuries. (2.) The Kshatrapah kings were, we know, preceded by at least one king of another race, who was destroyed
by an Andhrabritya king from the south, and both he and the
Kshatrapah kings show traces of the previous Greek domination
in the legends of their coins, and even, to some extent, in their
earliest types. (3.) The Kshatrapahs again were pretty certainly
succeeded by the later Guptas, somewhere about the ninetieth
year of the latter, or a little earlier, during the reign of Chandra
Gupta II. (4.) From the fourth Kshatrapah king after
Chastana (I do not quote Jiva Damnas date, which may be

nearly equivalent era), then the whole of the Gupta kings
would have been reigning parallel and contemporary
with the Kshatrapah kings, whose series comes down to at
least 304 of their era, for 304—57 = 247, and 78 + (Skanda Gupta's latest date) 146 = 224 only, whereas it can
scarcely be doubted from numismatic evidence that the
Guptas *followed* the Kshatrapahs. The Vikramáditya era
if applied to Gupta dates would of course bring out results
still more opposed to probability. It follows then the
Guptas must have used some special era of their own an-
terior to the Valabhi era, and this is really the point at
issue. It is not necessary to inquire how a writer of
Albirúni's curious accuracy was led into error, for there
can be no doubt of his meaning, though in some MSS. of
his work the statement is coupled with an expression
which indicates that the author was not himself quite

---

doubtful) to the latest, a period from 72 to 304 of their era
elapsed, and their last king possibly reigned later still, for he
had only been four years on the throne then, and as his grand-
father ceased to reign only one year before his accession, he
cannot have been old in 304. Nahapána, the only known
king of the dynasty who preceded them, was reigning in the
year 46 of that or some closely equivalent era. (5) Now there
is hardly any time into which the long period of over 260 years
of peaceful rule will fit in the history of Western India, *after*
the Greek domination, except the earliest centuries of the
Christian Era. And of the Kshatrapah kings I am in a position
to say from dated coins that the fourth, fifth, and sixth kings
together reigned at least sixty-nine years ; Rudra Séna, the son
of Vira Damna the sixteenth king after Chastana, reigned full
eighteen years. Swami Rudra Sena, son of Swami Rudra Damna
the antepenultimate king, reigned at least twenty-seven years,
and several other kings had reigns of ordinary duration, the
seventeenth, eighteenth, and nineteenth reigning, for example,
twenty-four years between them—say, eight years apiece.
Such a duration of reigns argues a long period of comparatively
peaceful rule hardly to be looked for, as already said, in Western
India except about the period named.

certain of its accuracy; he was probably put in the
wrong by his informants, but whence their mistake arose
is less easy to say, and is indeed hardly material.

The question of the Valabhi dates themselves bears
more immediately on the general question, for we now
possess a series of dates distributed pretty closely over
sixteen of the recorded kings of that dynasty, beginning
with the fourth and ending with the nineteenth. The
first king was father of the succeeding four, and the
earliest date employed by the fourth king is 207, though
he reigned some years later also.

It is palpable that this date cannot be applied to any
era beginning with the foundation of the dynasty, for it
is impossible that two generations should be spread
over two centuries, while the genealogy is so often repeated in the inscription that there can be no possible
mistake on this point.

If again these dates be applied to the Valabhi era of
319 A.D., they would bring down the later kings of the
dynasty past the middle of the eighth century, for their
dates reach to 447. At the close of that century or shortly
afterwards arose, as we know, the Chawára kings, and the
interval would not suffice for the intermediate reigns of
the many kings whose dated copper plates are extant.
Besides it is improbable that if the Valabhi kings had
the selection of their own era, that they would have
chosen one having an origin so distinct from their own,
and therefore most certainly referring to some event un-
connected with their rise.

Albirúni (as well as tradition) informs us that the
Guptas immediately preceded the Valabhis. The tradition recorded by Major Watson, though contradicted by
the inscriptions in some respects and improbable in

d

others, contains two points which are quite consistent
with the inscriptions, and as to one indeed is directly
supported by them.   These statements are to the effect
that the family of the Valabhi kings was founded by a
subordinate of the Guptas ; and, secondly, that they made
themselves practically independent two years before the
death of *Skanda* Gupta, and avowedly so soon after that
event.

That the earlier kings at least, if not all of the race,
owned some sort of superior authority has long since
been shown by Dr. Bühler from the language of the inscriptions themselves.   Not to multiply references, the
following quotation expresses his views—views which on
other grounds seem to be at least probable.   Writing on
a Grant of Dharaséna I., Ind. Ant. 1877, p. 9, he says :—
" In my article on the Grant of Dharaséna I., of Samvat,
216, I pointed out that this maharája was certainly the
vassal of some greater king ; and that Dronasinha's boasted
coronation had not raised him much above the position
which his predecessors, the two sénapatis or generals,
occupied . . . . I will now express my belief that eventually we shall find it proved that the Valabhi dynasty
was at no period free from vassalage, except perhaps
during the reign of Dharaséna IV., who calls himself
' King of kings, Chakravartin, Emperor, and Supreme
Lord.' "

I may add that one copy of the " Mirát-i-Ahmadi,"
a local history of Gujerát (a very fine copy),[17] expressly

---

[17] This copy is the property of Rao Bahadur Bholanath
Suratni.   It seems to have been made from an original, pre-
pared by the author with a special preface, as a presentation
copy for the chief who was Soubadár of Gujerát at the date of
its publication.

asserts that Gujerát was subject to the Kanouj kings *till* 812, (*in one copy*, 802) *Vikraméditya*. This work is no doubt of comparatively late date, but it was locally and very carefully compiled, and there can be little doubt that this statement, though I have not yet been able to trace it further, is made on good authority. If this be so, the assertion of the tradition that Bhatarka, the founder of the Valabhi race, was originally a deputy of the Gupta kings, seems *primâ facie* likely, and the Valabhis may afterwards have owned a more or less nominal dependence on the Kanouj kings, such as the Soubadárs of Oudh, Bengal, and the Dekhan owed to the throne of Dehli during the decadence of the Moghul Empire.

If this be so, there is no inherent improbability in the fact stated in Major Watson's tradition, that the Valabhi Bhatarka became independent about two years before Skanda Gupta's death, which was probably a period of weakness, for the greatness of the Gupta kingdom almost entirely ceased at his death.[18]

These facts then would all be in consonance with the continued existence of an acknowledged subordination, more or less real, to the Kanouj rulers for the time being; a subordination which would not improbably have induced the Valabhi kings to continue the unchanged use of the Gupta era.

If this be so, then 207 of the Gupta era would put the latest known date of the fourth king down to sixty-one years after the death of Skanda Gupta (placing that in 146 of the Gupta era), and sixty-three years after the independence of Bhatarka, the father of this king, in

---

[18] I have, since writing the above, come across Major Watson's paper in the "Indian Antiquary," vol. iii. p. 41, which confirms the fact above stated on other authority.

accordance with Major Watson's tradition. No doubt
this is a long period to allow for an interval of only two
generations, but not an impossible one,[19] particularly in a
polygamous nation, where brothers are often of a very
unequal age. With the exception of this point there
seems no other chronological objection to the adoption of
the Gupta era by the Valabhi kings, as General Cunningham, and, I believe, Dr. Bühler also, have long since
recognised.

But it may be asked what then was the Valabhi era
of 319 A.D., the existence of which rests not only on
Albirúni's authority, but at least on the evidence of one
inscription and of universal tradition ? As has been
shown, it cannot in any case have been that which was
commonly employed by the Valabhi kings themselves.
It may have taken its rise, for example (as some tradition
asserts), from the foundation of the new city of Valabhi.
I venture to suggest another *possible* date, viz., the death
of Kumára Gupta.[20] This apparently took place in the

---

[19] The interval from our own George III.'s accession to the
death of his son William IV. was seventy-seven years. Bhatarka
in all probability was somewhat older than George III. at his
accession, for he held official rank before it ; the fourth king
reigned for several years, and the fifth king was also his son ; but
this last probably reigned a very short period, as his name is
omitted altogether in some of the genealogies. On the other
hand, the Duke of Sussex survived his brothers several years.

[20] It is not proposed to *insist* on the date of Kumára Gupta's
death as that of the initiation of the Gupta era. According
to Major Watson's tradition there was an interval of two years
between the virtual and the avowed independence of the Valabhi
ruler. See "Arch. Survey Report," vol. ix. fig. 3, pl. v. General
Cunningham is inclined to assign some of the rude coins, to
which allusion has been made as probably posthumous, to a *son*
of Kumára Gupta, other than Skanda Gupta, and it may well be
that the Valabhi ruler for a time put forward the name of some
puppet of the Gupta race to cloak his own ambitious objects.

year 130 of the Gupta era, for a coin of his dated 130 is published by General Cunningham in vol. ix., "Arch. Survey of India," p. 24; and his successor seems to have ascended the throne the same year. ("Arch. Survey," vol. ix. p. 21, Thomas's "Dynasty of the Guptas," p. 55.) If the Valabhi kings rebelled against Skanda Gupta, having been before vassals of Kumára Gupta, they may have professed to ignore the former altogether;[21] and in support of such a theory it may be said that there was a very large issue of rude coins in Kumára Gupta's name, but of the general style and execution of the Valabhi coins. These Dr. Bühler has already, on purely numismatic grounds, recognised as a *posthumous coinage* struck by the Valabhis after Kumára Gupta's death. Of course, this assumption would exactly throw back the initial date of the Gupta era, as already suggested, to 189 A.D., which is well within the possible limits already assigned in the beginning of this paper, and which, as has been shown, fits other facts sufficiently well. An earlier date would suit, perhaps, better with the end of the Kshatrapah, a later one with the beginning of the Kábul dates; but in either case there exists no great difficulty in the hypothesis.

Certainly the early part of Skanda Gupta's reign would seem to have been a period of civil war—and unsuccessful civil war according to his inscription on the Bhitari Lát. ("Journal Royal Asiatic Society," Bo. Branch, vol. x. p. 59), but I *prefer* the date 189 A.D., though it may be either late or too early. Of course this would make the period occupied by the four first Valabhi kings some sixteen years longer. But this is still not impossible.

[21] It seems at least not improbable that the Valabhi era, though no doubt known and recognised, was not one which ever came into general use; one or at most two inscriptions mention it, and even then merely as the equivalent of another era, and they are of late date. It was not improbably a courtier's era, much like Akbar's Ilahi era.

I feel, however, bound also to notice the views on this question which have necessarily been advanced by writers whose account demands respect. Professor Oldenburg, in a paper recently published in the "Zeitschrift für Numismatik," and reprinted in the "Indian Antiquary," attributes to the Kshatrapah kings an era of their own, and holds the Kanishka dynasty of Indo-Scythians to have originated the Sáka era, beginning 78 A.D. Now as their dates show that they reigned for at least ninety-eight years, he considers that this last fact necessitates a much later period for the Guptas, who succeeded them (and who succeeded also the Kshatrapahs), on account of the great state of degradation into which the coinage of these Indo-Scythians, more or less gradually, passed. This last argument is no doubt a perfectly legitimate one, but the facts on which it is founded are capable of an explanation consistent with an assignment of an earlier date to the Guptas.

Indeed these facts as regards the *gold* coinage of the Indo-Scythians in India "intra Gangem," are hardly correctly stated. The best types of the Indian gold coinage of the Indo-Scythians pass almost without break into the gold coinage of the Guptas.

Gold Indo-Scythian coins of a more degraded type do no doubt occur, but the experience of Indian collectors, if consulted, will show that these are found almost exclusively in the Punjáb, or at any rate in the country to the north of the Jumna River, a tract to which the *direct* sovereignty of the Guptas almost certainly did not extend. It is true that the Gupta kings boast, in their inscription, that the kings as far as the Yaudhéyas (the people of the Panjáb salt range) were tributary to them; and this may have been the case. But there is, so far as I am aware, no evidence whatever to establish their direct rule so far

to the north; on the contrary, the Indrapúra grant, of
146 Gupta, only claims for them the "Antarved," that
is the country between the Ganges and the Jumna. The
Vishnu Purána assigns to them only Magadha and the
country along the Ganges to Prayág (Allahabad); and
while other authorities extend their territories as far to
the east as Sakéta, there is no mention anywhere of their
possessions comprising any part of the country north of
the Jumna, which river was, therefore, probably the
extreme upper limit of their direct rule. The country
beyond that river seems to have been for a time, at least,
in the hands of kings of Indo-Scythian descent, or of
kings who had adopted Indo-Scythian types of coinage,
though this part of the numismatic history of India has
scarcely yet been fully examined.

The copper coinage of the Indo-Scythians no doubt, as
pointed out by Professor Oldenburg, suffered, even in the
country once held by the Guptas, extreme degradation,
such as probably required a considerable period of time
to effect, but it does not follow that this time must have
elapsed *before* the Gupta rule began. It is to be remem-
bered that the Gupta kings seem hardly to have coined in
copper at all. Copper coins of only one or two of these
kings have been found, and these are among the rarest of all
Indian coins; moreover, so far as I am aware, they seldom
occur except in the immediate neighbourhood of the Gupta
capital, Kanouj. Whence, then, it may be asked, under
Gupta rule, came the supply of copper money which the
necessities of the country no doubt demanded? The
answer may fairly be obtained from a review of what has
happened under English rule in India. It is only, it may
be said, within the last fifty years that any attempt has
been made to supply an adequate and authoritative copper

currency ; and, meanwhile, not only have petty princes in independent states coined with all sorts of devices, but even bankers at large centres of trade, *e.g.*, at Gorakhpúr and Jagádhri, have supplied rude copper tokens which pass current to this day, and are even in some places still preferred to the neat Government coinage.

Under such a state of things an imitation of the current types would be only natural, and would doubtless eventually, though gradually, result in very crude caricatures of the original model. The deterioration, therefore, of the Indo-Scythian coinage probably went on, not only before the accession of the Guptas, but under, and even possibly after them. And assuming the Kanishka dynasty to have arisen in 78 A.D., and to have continued for about one hundred years, a position which I am not, at present at any rate, concerned to dispute, there is nothing in this fact, at least on numismatic grounds, and I am aware of no others, to militate against the initiation of Gupta rule some time during the two latter decades of the second century A.D.

General Cunningham, in the last published volume of the "Archæological Survey," approaches the subject rather from the point of view adopted in this paper, but is now disposed, chiefly on the strength of certain astronomical calculations, to place the date of the Gupta era earlier by some twenty or thirty years than has been suggested by myself.

Unfortunately these calculations are so beset on every side with chances of error that it is wholly impossible to accept them when they conflict with other trustworthy testimony; for example, when an eclipse is mentioned it is rarely certain whether the date given refers to the eclipse itself, to the date of the execution of the grant, or

to some other fact. In some cases, as in that of the
Morbi Grant, it is impossible that the date can refer, as
it stands, to the eclipse which it records.[22] Again, it
is very doubtful to what degree of accuracy the methods
of the older Indian astronomers, or of any particular
astronomer, attained ; and certainly several local differences in the mode of calculation existed. When to
these sources of error in ancient days are added those
of modern calculators, not perhaps perfectly versed in
all the ancient modes of working, the chances of error
are indefinitely multiplied. The extremely conflicting
results brought out from time to time from the same
data are in themselves such as to shake all faith in the
value of this source of information. Indeed, there is
nothing further to add to what is said on this point by
Mr. Thomas in pp. 542, 543, vol. xiii. J.R.A.S. (N.S.).

General Cunningham, however, relies on another piece
of evidence, which, though it hardly conflicts with the
data assumed in this paper, may be stated briefly thus :
Samudra Gupta claims to have received tribute from "Daiva
pútra sháhán sháhi;" this was the title of the Indo-
Scythians of the Kanishka race ; this race was identical
with the Yuechi of the Chinese historians. According to
the latter the Yuechi put their kings to death, and were

---

[22] In *Knowledge* of June 9th, 1882, pp. 26, 27, is a paper on
the Babylonian calendar, which shows several eclipses recorded
on similarly " impossible " monthly dates. The fact is explained by the hypothesis that the year consisted of twelve
equal months of thirty days each, with an intercalary month
every sixth year. Perhaps this was the model of the Gupta
year. See grant of Dharaséna II., " Ind. Antiquary," vol. vii.
p. 69, which gives a date of the *fifteenth* day of the " dark " half
of the month (of course " dark " would be a misnomer) ; but
if this be so, we have still much to learn of Indian eras before
we can apply astronomical tests with accuracy.

afterwards ruled by military chiefs, sometime between 220 and 280 A.D., Samudra Gupta therefore must have reigned before the kings were put to death. Admitting that no other race used the title of " Daiva pútra sháhán sháhi," and that the Kanishka Indo-Scythians were meant by the Chinese under the title of Yuechi ; and, further still, that these military chiefs did not arrogate to themselves the high-sounding title quoted, all of which points may be open to doubt ; still, all that can be said is that under the very latest date suggested above for the Gupta era, viz. 200 A.D., Samudra Gupta's reign, which ceased in or before the eighty-second Gupta year, will fall almost, if not entirely, in the interval—220 to 280 A.D.

On the other hand this evidence is of value, as it confirms the probability of the existence during the Gupta rule, of an Indo-Scythian dynasty in the Punjáb or thereabouts, which has been already inferred from independent facts.

In conclusion, it may be said that, although it cannot be hoped that the vexed questions of ancient Indian chronology, with which this paper deals, are fully determined ; and if views have been hazarded regarding them which are directly at variance with the conclusions of skilled and experienced writers—yet this has been done because there are new data which seemed to deserve examination and an attempt to reconcile them with the whole of the known facts ; I venture, therefore, to submit the results to which this has led me, in the hope that the discussion may at least help towards a satisfactory decision of the points at issue.

DESCRIPTIVE LIST OF COINS ENGRAVED.

1. Copper. British Museum. Weight 30.3 grs.

Obv. Peacock with outstretched wings, as on Gupta coins; dotted marginal circle. Degraded execution and poor preservation.

Rev. Lion of Varka's type to the left.

Legend श्री कमर ..? Srí Kamara ..? or Kamra?

2. Copper. My cabinet. Weight 33 grs.

Obv. Elephant (as on Varka's coins) to the left; rude execution.

Legend श्री पद्म ..? Srí Padama ..? Pakma? Vakama?

Rev. Lion to the right. Spirited execution. Mono. ट? D..?

3. Silver. E.I. Office.

Obv. Bull Nandi.

Legend श्री खलपति ... Srí Syalapati (Deva).

Rev. Horseman to right; in front of horse the

Legend ... गुप्र:? ? Gupta ...?

4. Silver. British Museum.

Obv. As on preceding coin.

Rev. Horseman in front of horse the

Legend ९८ गुप्र (?) 98 Gupta- (sya?).

5. Similar coin. British Museum.

Rev. Legend ९९ गु ..: 99 Gu ..?

6. Group of letters representing the word "Gupta."

7. Similar coin to fig. 5. My cabinet. Very poor preservation.

Rev. Legend ७०७: 707.

8. Similar coin. My cabinet.[23]

Rev. Legend ७२७: 727.

---

[23] This is only a cast; it is given, nevertheless, because the figures are more distinct than on most of the genuine coins, of which, however, there are several of this date both in the British Museum and in the India Office.

9 and 10. Similar coins. E.I. Office.

11. Silver. Mr. C. J. Rodgers.

Obv. As on the preceding coins.

Rev. Horseman with Arabic legend in front of horseman (con-
jecturally) ? ? رعايۃ المحمد عالی áli al Mahomed
riyayat ? ? رعايۃ المحمد لۃ عليۃ álayut li al Mahomed
riyayat ? ?

12 and 13. Two similar coins. British Museum.

14. Silver. Bibliothèque Nationale, Paris.

Obv. Bull Nandi.

Legend المقتدر بللۃ Al Muktadir billah; Mono. ड? th.

Rev. A horseman to the left without spear.

Legend جعفر للۃ Lillah Jaffir.

15. Copper. My cabinet. (Devices in outline.) Wt. 24.3 grs.

Obv. Elephant (as on Varka's coins) to left.

Legend श्री समन्त देव Sri Samanta Deva.

Rev. Lion to right.

Legend (over lion) ? ? المتقی Al Mutaki (billah?).

16. Similar coin. My cabinet (poor preservation). Wt. 50 grs.

Rev. Legend (over lion) Arabic undeciphered.

17. Silver. British Museum.

Obv. Bull Nandi.

Legend श्री क्रदवयकः Sri khvadayakah.

Rev. Horseman. Mono. म? "ma?" and عدل "adil:" in a
species of toghra a date ८१४? 814?

18. Similar coin. British Museum. Of ruder execution and
with a monogram undeciphered below the horseman.

19. Silver. British Museum.

Obv. Bull Nandi.

Legend श्री भीम दे . . Sri Bhíma D(eva).

Rev. Horseman. Mono. भी and म ? "bhí" and "ma." Date
᠀ᓯᶠ 814.

20. Similar coin. E.I. Office. Mono. भी "bhí," and rude
imitation of عدل "adal." Date ᠀ᓯᶠ 814.

21. Silver coin. My cabinet. (Poor preservation.)

Obv. Bull Nandi.

Legend श्री समन्त देव Srí Samanta Deva.

Rev. Horseman to right.[24]

Legend محمد "Mahomed" over horse's head. Date
᠀ᓯᶠ 814.[25]

22. Similar coin (my cabinet), but with the name مسعود
"Masaúd" substituted for that of Mahomed.

23. Similar coin (Mr. Rodgers), with the name مودود "Módúd"
substituted for that of Mahomed.

24. Similar coin, but without Arabic legend, of late execution.
E.I. Office. Date ᠀᠂ᓯ गु 802 "Gu."

[26] 25, 26, 27. Similar coins. My cabinet. Dated ᠀ᓯᓯ गु 812
"Gu." Mono. टट ? tt ?

28. Similar coin. My cabinet. Dated ᠀ᓯᓯ 813. Mono. क ? ka ?

[26] 29, 30, 31. Similar coins. My cabinet. Dated ᠀ᓯᶠ. Mono.
भी and عدل "adal."

---

[24] Attention may be drawn to the horseman's spear, which,
instead of the pointed head, bears a ring such as is used for play-
ing the game of chougán; probably some sarcasm is implied.

[25] The dates on all the individual Ghaznevide coins engraved
show no figures clearly save only the numeral 4, but a numerous
series in the cabinet of Mr. C. J. Rodgers shows that the true
reading in all cases must be that given above.

[26] The coins with the dates ᠀ᓯᓯ Gu. and ᠀ᓯᶠ are rather common and are found with varying monograms. I have one of the
latter with the monogram टट and in the British Museum the
monograms म and गु likewise occur in connection with these
dates.

32. Similar coin. My cabinet. Date ᴧɪᴄ 815. Mono. عدل "adal."

33. Similar coin. E.I. Office. Dated ᴧɪᴠ 817. Mono. illegible.

34. Copper. My cabinet. Probably of Kangra dynasty. Weight 51 grs. Rude copy of preceding type. Date before horse ᴧɪꜰ 814.

35. Similar coin (in my cabinet). Weight 51.25 grs.

This coin is of very degraded type. The figure of the bull may be made out on the obverse, but with no legend; the hind quarters only of the conventional horse are given on the reverse with the date ᴧᴧꝙ 886.[27]

---

[27] The weights only of the new copper types published are given above. The silver coins are all apparently of the Kábul standard, which Mr. Thomas considers to be about 48 grains. The average of selected specimens I found to be about 51 grs. and some reach to 52; their original weight may have been a little higher still.

The equivalents of the early dates are, to distinguish them, given in the above list in *Hindi* numerals,—those of later dates in *Arabic* numerals.

35 looks like the common emblem of Siva, to be found everywhere in India, Mahadeo ec ar Elephanta near Bombay and at the Tunk near the west The Sunhars decem- As some early called T

POSTSCRIPT TO THE PAPER ON THE DATES FOUND ON HINDU KABUL COINS.

By SIR E. CLIVE BAYLEY, K.C.S.I.

SINCE the above paper was in print I have had the advantage of conversing with Professors Oldenberg and Jacóbi, and find that they both attach more value than has been allowed in my argument, to the astronomical evidence cited by General Cunningham. Professor Jacóbi has himself recalculated the tables which General Cunningham received from Pandit Bápú Déva Shástri, and considers them to be correct. He, however, pointed out to me that, according to these tables, the year 190 A.D. will suit the dates given by General Cunningham quite as well as 167 A.D., which General Cunningham has adopted as the commencement of the Gupta era.

On examining this point more closely, I find that, as a matter of fact, the year 190 suits far better, agreeing exactly with three out of the five dates given, and in the other two the differences can be corrected by supposing a slight and very probable error.

General Cunningham's argument is founded on the employment in certain cases of dates in the Gupta era, *together* with dates also in the Vrihaspati or Jovian cycle, in which the years are named after the twelve months of the Hindu year, but the name of one of the months is dropped every eighty-sixth year in order to make the *cycle* years

a

accord with the actual years of Jupiter's revolutions.
Bápú Déva Shástri has given a table of the Vrihaspati
era rendered into years of the Christian era, which General
Cunningham has quoted in vol. x. of the "Archæological
Survey Report;" and the results of applying this to the
dates of five inscriptions quoted, according to the two
dates 167 A.D. and 190 A.D. respectively, will be now given.

There is a sixth inscription which, though not giving
the Jovian date, gives the day of the week. General
Cunningham relies much on this date, which will also be
tested.

The dates of the inscriptions will be found at pp. 9 to 16
of vol. ix. of the "Archæological Survey of India," and
these, according to the initial year 167 A.D., come out as
follows:—

    I. 156. Máha Vaisákh, 156 + 167 A.D. = 323 A.D. (Bápú
        Déva gives Jyestha).
    II. 173.[1] Máha Aswayuja, 173 + 167 A.D. = 340 A.D. (B. D.
        gives Kartik).
    III. 188. Máha Margasira, 188 + 167 A.D. = 355 A.D. (B. D.
        gives Margasira).
    IV. 191. Máha Chaitra, 191 + 167 A.D. = 358 A.D. (B. D.
        gives Vaisákh).
    V. 209. Máha Aswayuja, 209 + 167 A.D. = 376 A.D. (B. D.
        gives Kartik.)

That is, the result tallies exactly only in the case of
No. III. inscription. With the initial date 190 A.D., however, the case is very different, as will be seen below:—

    I. 156. Máha Vaisákh, 156 + 190 A.D. = 346 A.D., which
        was Máha Vaisákh.
    II. 173. Máha Aswayuja, 173 + 190 A.D. = 363 A.D., which
        was Máha Aswayuja.
    III. 188. Máha Margasira, 188 + 190 A.D. = 378 A.D., which
        was Máha Vaisákh.

---

[1] This date is 163 in the original plate, but, as Gen. Cunningham points out, it is a palpable error for 173.

IV. 191. Máha Cháitra, 191 + 190 A.D. = 381 A.D., which
was Máha Cháitra.
V. 209. Máha Margasira, 209 + 190 A.D. = 399 A.D., which
was Máha Kartik.

It will thus be seen that 167 A.D. gives only one date
which exactly corresponds, two which are out by one
year, and two wholly wrong. On the other hand, 190 A.D.
gives three out of five cases exactly right, and in the
other two the dates are only out by one year, in one instance a year in defect, in the other a year in advance,
which might well be errors of a half-informed pandit
dealing with an unusual subject. Perhaps, considering all
the chances of error, this is as close an approximation to
astronomical precision as is to be expected in Indian
dates. It may be said that an additional source of con-
fusion has been pointed out to me by Professor Jacóbi,
viz., that some writers count an era from the first day
of what we should call the first year, while others, using
the same era, consider the first day of the era to be the
first after the first completed year. Again, the year may
commence at various seasons, according to local custom,
as in the case of the Vikramaditya era, which differs by six
months according to northern or southern usage.

The sixth date quoted by General Cunningham is that
of the Budha Gupta inscription of the 165th era, at Eran,
which is dated on *Thursday*, the 12th day of Ashadha.
According to the date of 167, Bápú Déva Shástri brought
out this date as a *Friday*, but General Cunningham, by
applying another and more ancient mode of reckoning,
brought out a correct result. Apparently, however,
according to the method given in Prinsep's[2] tables (Prinsep, *Essays*, ed. Thomas, vol. ii., pp. 180, 181), the 12th

[2] By these tables the date seems to be Thursday, 17th May,
355 A.D.

Ashadha, 355 A.D. (165+190), *was Thursday*, and this too would agree with Bápú Déva's results. ✗

In four cases, therefore, if the last calculation be correct 190 A.D. gives exactly the results required by the inscriptions, and in the remaining two the approximation is so close that it may be practically neglected, especially as the error is in defect in one instance and in excess in the other.

Under these circumstances it may be better to take 190 A.D. rather than 189 A.D. as the real commencement of the Gupta era. Deducting this from 319 A.D., the date of the Valabhi era, it will give 129 of the Gupta era as the initial year of this last. If this be the date of Kumára Gupta's death, as has been suggested, then the coin dated 130, figured in vol. ix. of the "Archæological Survey Report," pl. v., fig. 7, must be taken as a posthumous one, which may well be the case, for the legend resembles that found on the ruder coins already described as posthumous. As regards other dates, 190 A.D. will fit as well as 189 A.D.

Mr. Burgess has, however, just informed me that the whole subject of the Jovian cycle is about to be reviewed by Mr. Thibaut, of Benares, in the "Indian Antiquary" for the month of September, 1882. These remarks are therefore given only "under reserve."

✗ This statement is erroneous but the real date is calculated by Professor Jacobi also comes out a Thursday

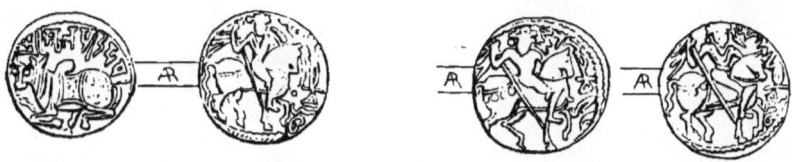

VALABHI SIGNS FOR HUNDREDS.

ᘔ = 100, ᘔᘔ = 200, ⅄ = 300, ⅄ = 400

COINS OF HINDU KINGS OF KABUL. PL. II.

T. T. Lees

www.ingramcontent.com/pod-product-compliance
Lightning Source LLC
Chambersburg PA
CBHW021558270326
41931CB00009B/1270